Balance Your Life:

Take Control of Your Time
Discover What Really Matters

Delores L. Mason

Delores L. Mason
1637 South Street
Philadelphia, PA 19146
267-939-8360
balancelifecoaching@comcast.net
www.2YourWell-Being.com

Limits of Liability and Disclaimer of Warranty

The author and publisher shall not be liable for your misuse of this material. This book is strictly for informational and educational purposes.

Warning – Disclaimer

The purpose of this book is to educate and entertain. The author and/or publisher do not guarantee that anyone following these techniques, suggestions, tips, ideas, or strategies will become successful. The author and/or publisher shall have neither liability nor responsibility to anyone with respect to any loss or damage caused, or alleged to be caused, directly or indirectly by the information contained in this book.

ISBN# 978-0-9844004-1-6

Dedication

Chance has not been set in stone.
There's meaning all around.
Open your Self to all life's gifts.
There's treasure to be found.

Delores L. Mason
Author

This book is dedicated to the
people who are my source of joy,
anxiety, love, frustration and support:
my family and friends.

I love you all dearly.

Acknowledgements

I want to thank my parents, Dean and Sophia, and my friends and family for their love, support and belief in me. I thank my mentors, coaches and teachers for helping me discover what I value most, and for giving me the tools to nurture those things. Their support has been invaluable, and their encouragement deeply appreciated. I also thank the people who have come to me for coaching. You have been an inspiration by teaching me through your own learning. Special thanks to Donna Kozik for her insight and motivation, and to Mari-Beth Geedey. Without the generous help of these individuals, this book would not have been possible.

Preface

Do you ever feel as though time is not on your side? When there's so much to do in any given day, do you wish you could clone yourself to get it all done? Maybe you've asked yourself: "When did I lose control of my time?" or "How can I regain balance in my life?"

Millions of us feel that our lives are no longer in balance—like we're dancing to someone else's tune instead of our own lovingly composed song. On top of working 40 or so hours per week, there are tasks and projects to tend at home, in the community and in your personal time.

I've worked in leadership development consulting and HR for over 14 years. My education is in organization and management development with a focus on individual well-being and positive work environments.

Because of my profession, I have spent years reading self-development books and articles, trying one solution then another. What I've learned is that the answers are out there, but they're also inside of you.

We're unique individuals in that what may work for one may not work for another. However, there are basic tenants that hold true for every one of us, and I want to share those with you in one convenient place—this book.

I generally introduce myself to new friends by smiling and saying "Hi, I'm Delores. I'm a writer, a life coach, a proud aunt, a good friend, and I'm passionate about treating animals and people with kindness, love and respect."

What I hope that greeting imparts to you is that I'm happy about who I am, what I do, and how I live my life. In those two lines of greeting, you get an idea of my values, what I choose to spend time doing, and what you can expect from me.

Uncovering those three things— your values, what you choose to focus your time on, and what others can expect from you—are crucial to taking control of your time, finding what really matters to you, and regaining balance in your life.

I became interested in finding balance when my life was spiraling out of control. I was mired in debt, my living situation was tenuous at best, my long-time job dissolved almost overnight, I could no longer afford college, and several friends had suddenly lost interest in being my friend.

I didn't have a substance abuse issue nor was I running from creditors or the law. So in perspective, my situation wasn't as dire as it could have been...as some people's lives are. However, it was enough for me to seek what I needed to regain balance in my life and experience less stress.

I read self-help books. I took up Tai Chi. I tried yoga. I even talked to a behavioral therapist. All good things, helpful things; but what stood out independent of them was the simple truth that I was the one who had to regain control of my time. I had to figure out what's important to me and start living in a way that made sense for me.

"It is difficult to see all the ingredients in the pot when you're stewing in your own soup."

The above quote is a humble nod to my own hard-earned wisdom. Sometimes it's difficult to see what's getting in your way because you're too close to the issue. This book will help you begin to see some of those obstacles.

You'll find I enjoy using cooking analogies. Cooking is one of my joys. It relaxes me and I find that creating something delicious and nourishing gives me confidence and personal satisfaction. It's one of the activities that I value and make time for in my life. That's what you'll discover for yourself through this book—what you value and want to make time to enjoy.

Granted, I'm no *Iron Chef*. I've created dishes I wouldn't feed to the dog, but I value the Zen and creativity of chopping, measuring, experimenting with flavors, testing, and tasting.

This book will help you begin to identify what you're passionate about and encourage you to embrace those things by letting go of the obstacles and time-hogs that keep you from doing what you enjoy most.

Some of us need more than what we'll find in any one book. A professional life coach can help you identify what you might need and what you might be doing that gets in the way of achieving your goal to find balance and well-being.

I've been fortunate to know several amazing individuals who have helped and continue to help me. Now, I enjoy being that resource for others.

As a coach, my interaction is one-on-one. Through this book, however, I hope to reach out to more people to share some personal wisdom about what is needed to balance your life.

I hope you find this book useful. Consider it your personal "pocket coach" and advisor for taking back control of your time and your life.

After you've read this book, I would love to hear your feedback and stories about what it's done for you. You can email me at: balancelifecoaching@comcast.net.

Delores

Table of Contents

Introduction

"Live a balanced life – learn some and think some and draw and paint and sing and dance and play and work every day some."

Robert Fulghum

I began my journey to find balance many years ago. Did I find it? Yes. Do I still occasionally lose it? Yes.

Balance is a skill, and like most skills it requires practice to maintain it. After all, if you stop playing tennis, you can't expect to leap onto the court after years of inactivity and play like you're one of the Williams sisters.

This book is a resource for whenever you're feeling out of sorts. Engage it whenever you need it. Reach for it regularly, and you'll find it easier to maintain harmony in your life.

What is Balance?

First, understand that balance is in every aspect of nature. We are beings that seek equilibrium in our lives, our work, our relationships and our play. Balance contributes to our well-being and health.

Did you ever spin around as a child until you were dizzy and lightheaded and everything around you spun out of control? Try to remember what that felt like. What can you recall?

I remember feeling as light as air then, as the world twirled out of focus, falling to the ground giddy and laughing until my stomach ached.

Now take a look around you. If you're in a clear, safe area then get up and spin around. Don't think about it. Just make sure you are in a safe area and then get up and spin around five to seven times.

How do you feel? Mentally scan your body and try to describe any sensations you experience. What expression did you have on your face when you began spinning? Did it change as you continued?

When I did this, I felt a little foolish—okay, a lot foolish—but by the first spin I was smiling and by the fifth spin I was laughing.

How was spinning as a child different from spinning just now? How is it the same? I didn't fall to the ground as I did when I was younger, but I did laugh and enjoy the experience.

This little exercise and your responses to the questions are very important in helping you find balance in your life.

When you took your first steps as an infant, you were off balance. You might have been bold and daring or uncertain and afraid.

Regardless, you kept at it. You practiced walking to find that balance. And you succeeded. It's likely that you were praised for it, and you felt good about yourself.

In physiological terms, when you spin around and stop, your sensory input improves for a brief moment. I like to think that children enjoy spinning because they find joy in losing balance and slowly regaining it. It's a cherished memory of learning to find balance all on your own.

Tapping into that memory can now serve a purpose. It can remind you that you *can* do this. You can find balance in your life again. All it takes is your willingness, awareness, motivation, and practice.

What You Can Expect to Achieve

This book will help you learn to regain balance in your life. I'll share quotes, stories and activities with you that will help you learn to identify what's taking up your time, what you need to let go of, and what you need to pay attention to in order to feel more well-rounded and balanced.

At times, you'll be asked to record what you're feeling, thinking and experiencing. Recording your thoughts, emotions and progress can be a vital step in making lasting change. It can help to make your situation concrete and real, and it can help you find the energy and motivation to move forward.

If engaging the activities suggested and journaling are all you do, you *can* find and begin to restore balance in your life. You can also take it a step further and share your learning and experiences with people you care about. Talking about your experiences can make them more concrete for you and help you make a commitment to making lasting changes that benefit your life. Finding a life coach is another option. The effective coach listens and advises you based on your specific needs, wants and challenges so that you succeed in your goals.

So let's begin.

Chapter 1: Embracing Sensation

"Why compare yourself with others?
No one in the entire world can do a
better job of being you than you."

Anonymous

I love this quote. It's a truism that applies to every one of us. You are unique— unlike no other in this world. So why, then do we find ourselves making comparisons to others?

Such comparisons can put us in a negative frame of mind and feed unhealthy emotions or beliefs such as "I'm not smart enough" or "I always mess things up." Conversely, if the comparison feeds our pride, then it gives us a false sense of superiority and feeds other unhealthy beliefs such as "I may not be the smartest person, but I'm smarter than him."

Does it really matter to you if you can't do something as well as others? If it does, then consider learning or practicing or doing what it takes to improve your skills. You have control over what you do, not what others do. Making comparisons like the ones above is unhealthy because there will always be someone better and someone not at your level. Instead, focus on where you are now and where you want to be.

Say this out loud:

"I am here because I am meant to be here."

Say it as many times as you need until you are comfortable with that phrase. Say it every time you feel out of balance and need reassurance that where you are is exactly where you need to be at that moment.

It's important to accept and appreciate where you are in your life...today...at this very moment.

No matter how chaotic or difficult your life path may seem, it has brought you to this awareness, so nothing has been in vain.

The Importance of Emotions

Sensation is how you become aware that *something* needs your attention. Learn not to run from your feelings, your emotions. You feel anxious, uncertain, sad or happy for a reason.

We are emotional beings. That's a simple fact. Whether you experience an event or interact with others, you respond emotionally first before your intellect kicks in to assess, interpret, and understand.

Emotions—especially so-called negative emotions—are your first signal that your conscious mind needs to wake up and pay attention. If you're feeling restless or anxious or nervous, you are out of balance, and your emotions are responding, giving you notice so you can move toward balanced awareness.

> "Just as your car runs more smoothly and requires less energy to go faster and farther when the wheels are in perfect alignment, you perform better when your thoughts, feelings, emotions, goals, and values are in balance."
>
> Brian Tracy, TV Host

Unlike motor vehicles, balance for humans begins from the inside out. We thrive when we are whole—when our minds, our bodies, our hearts, our spirits, and the bonds we share with others are supported, attuned, and being nourished properly.

If even one of those parts isn't being attended to, you might feel something isn't quite right.

Recognizing When You Are Out of Balance

Holism: (from the Greek *holos*, meaning all, total)

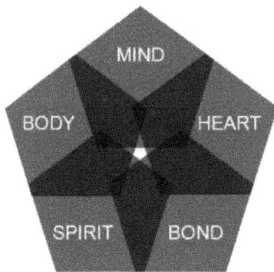

One cannot be determined or explained by component parts alone.

The whole determines how the parts behave.

Perhaps you are familiar with the holistic medicine wheel that addresses mind, body, heart and spirit. I've included "Bond" because your relationships—the bonds you form with others—are as vital a part of who you are and deserve to be included in your holism.

When your relationships or bonds are suffering, your overall well-being will manifest the imbalance in other aspects of your Self, just as when your emotions or physical being are out of balance.

*[Notice that I distinguish between **self** (the individual) and **Self** (holistic human being interacting with other human beings).]*

Many people are accustomed to relying heavily on one or a few aspects of the Self. Some focus on developing their minds and relationships, but neglect their emotional well-being. Some attend to emotional and physical presence—meaning how others perceive you—and neglect developing relationships or what feeds their spirit.

True balance requires your self attending to each area of the Self. You can begin to recognize that you may be out of balance by paying attention to the sensations you experience. Emotions that don't feel right, physical aches, strained relationships and scattered thoughts are sensations or alerts that you might be out of balance.

When you do feel those sensations, resist the temptation to leap straight into deep thought about what it might mean. Do not take random action just to ignore or get rid of the feeling, ache or random thoughts. Your Self is giving you a message. If you sit quietly with that sensation for a moment and allow yourself to feel what you are feeling, you can avoid leaping to a conclusion before you have all the facts.

Imagine preparing a recipe and discovering that you don't have any onions. You can go ahead and make the dish without the onions, but it will certainly produce a different flavor for the final dish. If you ignore sensations and rush headlong into a solution, you'll produce a different solution and may not end up where your Self is suggesting you need to be.

Sensation can be uncomfortable for you when you are unaccustomed to paying close attention. The more you practice mentally scanning your holistic Self, the more at ease you'll become with your emotions and thoughts.

When you sit with sensation, scan your body without judgment. For example, if your leg is twitching from nervousness, let it twitch for a moment. Ask yourself: What else am I experiencing? Is my pulse steady or a little rapid? Are my palms chilled and clammy or warm and dry? Is it difficult to focus my thoughts or am I hyper-focused on only one thought?

These sensations are present for a reason. Feel them. Pay attention to the sensation, then pick up a notebook or open a new Word document and jot down the date, time and what you notice about your emotions, your body and your thoughts.

Of course, if your physical sensation is extreme, don't hesitate to seek professional help. This process for finding balance does not belie the fact that serious threats to your health reveal themselves as chronic aches and pains. If you ever suspect a sensation underlies a more serious health threat, immediately seek medical attention.

When you journal, don't censor your writing. This process is for you, and you don't have to share it if you choose not to. Be as detailed as you can in your descriptions, as though you are outside your own body making observations.

It's a good idea to start keeping a Feelings Journal. As I stated in the Introduction, recording your thoughts, feelings and experiences can help to make it more real for you, more concrete, and over time you can begin to identify patterns you might not have observed because each occurrence is disconnected in your mind.

It's similar to glancing at the sundry items in your refrigerator or pantry and thinking: "I don't have anything to make for dinner." Without a written recipe with a list of ingredients in front of your eyes, you might not think that two lemons, a package of chicken thighs, mayonnaise, linguini and onions could lead you to create a wholesome, very tasty Chicken Pasta Salad.

So, do not run from sensations or your emotions. You want to face them, pay attention to them, and write them down.

The more you practice scanning your sensations, especially in light of finding your life overwhelming and out of balance, the sooner you can start to become aware of what's really in need of your attention.

Sensation leads to awareness when you allow yourself to experience those feelings and take note of when, how, and where those emotions rise up for you.

Chapter 2: Being Aware

"What is necessary to change a person is to change his awareness of himself."

Abraham Maslow

Margaret's Story

Margaret had a job she loved. She and her husband Greg were planning a second honeymoon in the fall. She decided to give up attending her Saturday gardening club to work overtime to earn a little extra so they wouldn't have to dip into their savings too much and their trip could be magical.

It seemed like a good plan, but one month later, Margaret was feeling really anxious. She was a little tired at the end of every workday, but she was in good health. Margaret ignored her anxiety, attributing it to her added hours at work.

Her anxiety didn't go away. In fact it grew.

One night she snapped at Greg for not taking out the garbage. They ended up arguing about other things as well. Alone in the bedroom, in tears, Margaret thought about their fight. Greg often forgot to take out the garbage in their ten years of marriage, so why did this time bother her so much?

At work, Margaret found it difficult to focus. More and more, little things that never bothered her before were igniting her temper, and soon Margaret was hard-pressed to remember why she was working so hard.

Finally, having had enough of her sullen, temperamental mood swings, Margaret talked to a friend, Susan, who coached divorcees through their emotional and tumultuous experience.

After a couple of conversations where Susan simply listened to Margaret and asked probing questions to get her talking more, Susan had Margaret make a list of all the changes she'd made in her life recently.

For each item Margaret listed, Susan had Margaret explore it more deeply. Here is their conversation about the gardening club that Margaret had given up.

"Tell me about the gardening club," Susan said.

"It's just a weekend thing I did because I enjoy gardening," Margaret replied.

"Why do you enjoy gardening?" Susan asked.

"I like being outdoors. It helps me relax."

"Why does it help you relax?"

After serious thought, Margaret said, "I don't know. I mean...well, I used to garden with my mother when I was a child. It was our time together. It was special."

"How was it special?"

"Well, we would plant flowers and talk and laugh. I have two older sisters. I love them, but that was just my time with Mom doing something that made me feel special."

"So you gardening made you feel special. You gave up gardening," Susan said. "What are you doing now that makes you feel special?"

Margaret had no answer for that question. However, by taking a closer look at the activities in her life and what they truly meant to her, Margaret began to realize that gardening was so much more than "just a weekend thing" as she'd initially stated.

Gardening was still a cherished time for herself. Working with plants and soil brought her peace of mind. It helped her connect with that feeling of being special.

She hadn't thought about what she was truly giving up when she decided to sacrifice her garden club to make extra money for the second honeymoon trip she and Greg were planning.

The Importance of Developing Self-awareness

Many of us live disjointed lives, paying little attention to all aspects of the Self. Like Margaret, you might sacrifice attending to one aspect of the Self—the spiritual self in her case—to put focus on something else. There's nothing wrong with doing that as long as you are truly aware of what you are doing and why you are doing it.

I often use "Why" questioning in my own coaching practice. It's a great way to get you focused and thinking beyond the responses that immediately come to your mind. It helps you develop your self-awareness.

Few of us spend time thinking about why we do the things that we do. Yet, developing your self-awareness is an important step in figuring out what is really important to you—what really maters.

When you experience sensation, allowing yourself to *feel* what's going on leads you to awareness. Exploring that awareness even further, leads to self-awareness: knowing who you are, how you think and feel, and accepting and loving who you are.

Self-awareness is necessary for you to make informed, healthy, holistic decisions. By knowing what you value, what you want to attain and where you are right now, you will be well-equipped to reach your goal of having more balance in your life.

Now vs. Ideal

When I work with individuals, I have them examine what their reality is now versus what an ideal reality would be in the near future. They can then identify steps to take to reach their goals.

Now vs. Ideal is a worksheet that can help you make a list of two to three repetitive activities you are currently doing in specific areas of your life, such as education, health, or family. In a parallel column, you will list two to three activities you would "love" to do in those areas. These would be activities or actions that fulfill you on a deeper level.

For example, I knew I wanted to get my Masters degree, but I didn't want to incur debt via student loans. That meant I would have to start saving money. To do that, I let go of a few current activities that were costing me such as eating out more than once a week, shopping for new clothes and purchasing kitchen gadgets, which I love to collect.

I started planning my meals, cooking more, and bringing my lunch to work. I put a limit of once every two weeks for meeting friends at restaurants, saving what would have otherwise been spent. I stopped buying clothing that wasn't essential and made do with existing cooking gadgets.

By creating my Now vs. Ideal list, I was able to see what I could let go of in the *Now* category in order to reach my *Ideal*. It took me three and a half years, but I saved and completed my degree with no debt, and I've gotten pretty darn good at cooking, if I say so myself.

There is always something you do now that you can release to make room for something more important. It could be a short-term trade-off or a permanent one if what you let go of isn't truly valued by you.

The worksheet for "Now vs. Ideal," and all other exercises mentioned in this book, can be found in the Appendix and on my website, www.2YourWell-Being.com, along with other valuable resources.

Giving visual substance (such as creating charts or list) to your current activities and desired activities helps you build awareness of what might be taking up your time and eating away at what you'd rather be doing.

Oftentimes, you get bogged down in a lot of "have-to's" when the reality is maybe you *don't* have to do that activity.

I'm a fairly organized person, but I loathe housework. I mean, I'd rather shovel elephant droppings three times a day than dust or vacuum or, heaven forbid, rake the backyard.

Yes, housework is a necessity, but how often is it a necessity? I know people who clean every day. If they enjoy it and it fulfills them in some way, more power to them.

For me, *"Swiffering"* bi-monthly works just fine. (That's every two weeks.) No one's ever come into my home and implied by words or actions that my place is not clean.

The point is a number of your "have-to's" might be either pre-conditioned notions, habits you learned from others or activities that no longer serve your needs. The real question then is: "What works for you now?"

My Juggling Act

You have things you are attending to and things you want to attend to but have allowed to fall by the wayside because it wasn't important or you already have too much on your plate. This isn't limited to actual, physical activities like housework or walking the dog. You have people, situations, problems and pressures you're juggling as well.

To help people become more self-aware of why they do what they do—or don't do—there's an exercise I've used called My Juggling Act. The worksheet is in the Appendix and available online.

On any given day when you're feeling overwhelmed by what feels like "have-to's", take a moment to think about the personal tasks, dilemmas and pressures facing you. Then fill each circle with those items; include everything in your daily picture that you to get a realistic view.

Creating a graphic depiction of what is taking up time in your day and what you can't seem to make time for can help you step back from the emotions (frustration, anxiety, etc.) attached to your daily schedule. When you engage your eyes, you activate parts of your brain that can dilute overwhelming emotions.

After writing your items, look at what you *are* juggling. Ask yourself *why* you need or want to juggle each particular item? What's the benefit to you if you keep that ball in the air today? What will happen if you let it go? Can you survive the day if you let it go? If you can't think of a personal benefit (such as peace of mind, better health, developing a stronger relationship, etc.), then that task might not be a "need to," and may not even be a "want to."

Next, look at what you are not juggling but it felt important enough to be placed on the worksheet. Ask yourself: Do I need or want to pick up that ball today? What benefit will I get by picking it up?

Setting Priorities

Once you are aware of what is on your plate or needs to be on your plate, getting your priorities clear is an essential step toward achieving a well-balanced life.

Important questions to ask are:

- What really matters to me?

- What do I really want to get out of this? Am I doing this because it makes me happy or because I think it's what I *should* do/ want/ need?

- If I could focus on one thing and one thing only today, what would that be? Why?

- If I could add a second or third thing, what would they be? Why?

When you are aware of what's important to you—what really matters in your life—you're prepared to make good decisions. You're ready to take control of your time and how you choose to spend it.

Awareness goes a long way toward finding the motivation and energy you need to make those lasting changes that will support your balanced life.

Chapter 3: Tapping into Energy

"People often say that motivation doesn't last. Well, neither does bathing - that's why we recommend it daily."

Zig Ziglar

Now that you've identified what is important to you, you are probably feeling excited and motivated to start making some changes. That's great! Motivation gives you the drive to move forward. It gives you energy that you can tap into to start living your life the way you've defined as mattering to you.

You will find energy to move forward just by having identified what is truly important to you. Anticipation and the promise of reward are often enough to get you up and moving.

However, the initial momentum—especially for a goal that might be fairly distant in the future—will likely taper off over time. That burst of energy you most likely felt when you first identified your new goal won't support a long-term thing like sustainable behavior change.

Making successful changes in habitual behaviors can take anywhere from 21 to 60 days to cement in your unconscious mind. That means that you have to sustain the new thought, belief or action regularly for approximately a month before it becomes second nature to you—and that doesn't include any set-backs or stumbles of old behavior along the way.

Developments in technology have conditioned people to expect instant gratification. It's amazing that you can go online, order a shoji screen from a manufacturer in Japan and have it in your home in a matter of days. Email has made it possible to communicate rapidly with people thousands of miles away. The Smartphone gives you fingertip access to the Internet. Unfortunately, your expectations and need to have instant gratification works counterintuitively when it comes to motivation and energy.

Sustaining the Energy and Motivation to Change

As the quote at the beginning of the chapter alluded, motivation may not last. However, there are things you can do to help maintain vigor and enthusiasm as you take control of your time.

Build a Network of Support

There's nothing like having your own cheering section to give you the encouragement you need to keep going forward. Your cheerleaders can be family, friends, colleagues, a life coach, or anyone who is supportive of your goal to find and maintain balance. Turn to these people when you feel an ebb in your energy.

You may also want to build a network of support in terms of getting some of your tasks done. Let's face it, there are chores and tasks that need attending; however, they don't necessarily have to be attended to by you.

Allow yourself to rely on your partner, family members, friends, co-workers, or neighbors—anyone who can watch the kids or handle an errand while you focus on some of your new goals. Bartering, or swapping favors, is a great way to free some of your time *and* strengthen your network of support.

If you enjoy making lists, then create a three-column list. In the first column, name the individuals in your network of supporters. In the second column, list a few ways each individual's talents, likes or interests might support your goal. In the third column, list how your talents, likes and interests can support and energize them in ways they may need.

Keep this list nearby and update it as you discover the hidden talents and interests of your friends, family and neighbors and meet more people to grow your network of support.

Let Go of Unimportant Things

A key to achieving and maintaining balance relies on your ability to let go of things that aren't a priority to you.

Either drop what's not essential, or find others who can take care of those items for you (consult your network of support). These unessential things keep you from doing what might otherwise matter more to you.

I shared with a friend that I took my two queen-size comforters to the neighborhood Laundromat and paid $40 to have them washed, dried and folded once a month. She looked at me as though daisies were sprouting on my head.

"But you have a washer and dryer," she said.

"Yes," I replied. "I could spend 30 or 60 minutes tackling that, but there are other things I'd rather be doing."

It's worth it to me to pay someone else to spend the time doing certain shores or tasks so I have more time to write, coach someone, visit with loved ones, or relax by having private time to search for new recipes and cook.

When my yard needs a good cleaning, I invite my nephews over for a free meal. They love to eat and don't mind raking and gathering leaves. I get to cook, spend time with family, and get a clean yard in the process.

The point is, I'm willing to let go of what's not important to me, or to barter my interests with others, so I have more time for what really matters.

If you find it difficult to start this process, discuss it with one of your supporters. Perhaps he/she can help you see things in a way that you haven't yet learned to embrace.

Do First Things First—Prioritize

Prioritizing can help you focus on the tasks that truly require your attention or that you know will inspire and nurture you. Tend first to the activities that relate closest to what is important to you. This can help you build up lots of energy and motivation to move on to the next thing, then the next, and so on.

If you use the Juggling Act worksheet in the Appendix to help you sort and prioritize, you can see what tasks, obligations or pressures are taking much of your time that are not a priority for you.

On the following page is a tool that you might also find useful. It involves assigning a level (high or low) of urgency and importance to any task or action.

	URGENT	NOT URGENT
IMPORTANT	**A**	**B**
NOT IMPORTANT	**C**	**D**

It's important to know that an item is considered "urgent" when there is an approaching deadline—whether self-imposed or externally created. For example, filling out a college application that must be submitted in two weeks has a high level of urgency. In comparison, filling out an application that's due in two months has a low level of urgency. Beginning a fitness regimen next week is urgent, whereas starting your regimen in three months is not urgent.

A task is "important" when it is something that matters to you. Something you personally value will rate high, whereas a task or activity that doesn't pique your interest will have a low level of importance.

Place the items from your My Juggling Act worksheet into the prioritizing grid, or create a to-do list and plug those into the appropriate squares based on their urgency and importance.

Items that fall into category "A" are your priority for the day and should be designated a "first things first" task. This is where you'll find the most energy and motivation for getting things done.

Items in category "B" are tasks that can shift into category "A" once tasks from that quadrant have been attended to. If you have more than four items in "B", you might want to consider bartering or swapping with your network of supporters.

Items that fall into category "C" are ideal for tapping your network of supporters. These items have a deadline attached, but don't spark your interest. Remember, what you don't find interesting, others might find engaging and be willing to trade to get accomplished.

Category "D" contains things you might actually be able to let go of to make more room and more time for what you are discovering as mattering most to you.

As you gain more balance in your life, you may find that the majority of your day-to-day tasks fall into category "B." This is ideal because that's the category that affords you the most flexibility and creativity in getting things done.

New priorities crop up unexpectedly. Don't let that frazzle you. Add it to your prioritizing grid and look at the other tasks. Is there anything you can put off until later or ask someone else to manage for you? With this new priority added, what no longer feels important or urgent to you?

Talk it through with someone if you find it difficult to shift your focus. You have the power to readjust your personal priorities. It's all a part of taking control of your time.

Schedule Relaxation

If you're like most people, you schedule nearly every aspect of your life; why not be more intentional in making sure you have the break you deserve?

Relaxation is an essential part of living a well-balanced life. I'm not talking about the importance of six to eight hours sleep. I'm talking about an intentional respite for yourself where you have the uninterrupted time to do whatever it is you find relaxing or rejuvenating.

Maybe it's reading another chapter of a good book, or getting a manicure or massage. Perhaps it's taking a stroll in the park, or sitting in the comfy chair at home and watching television.

You are in control of your time. Taking a moment to relax and tend to your mind, body, heart, spirit and relationships ensures that you're well-fed and prepared for anything.

Get into the habit of taking time for your Self. I capitalize the word here because it's important to distinguish a respite that nurtures you emotionally, physically, or spiritually. As little as 20 minutes of uninterrupted time doing something just for you, can go a long way toward reviving your energy.

Make a list of things you do or would like to do to relax and de-stress. Include realistic activities you can anticipate over the next couple of weeks. Then sprinkle one into your schedule every day or every other day. You can generate lots of energy by simply knowing that you have a treat to look forward to in the day or during the week.

A Formula to Increase Your D.R.I.V.E.

There's a formula I created that I use for myself, and with individuals I've coached, that helps to stay focused and ensure an easy tapping into of energy whenever needed.

Decide – Identify what really matters and what doesn't.

Release – Let go of what doesn't really matter to you.

Inform – Turn to your network of supporters to barter tasks or get encouragement.

Value – Have confidence that your personal work is adding value to you and everyone who matters to you.

Engage – Take action.

This formula works well for individuals who favor logic and making associations rather than visual charts or lists. Try the exercises suggested to find out what works best for you. Often, just having clarity is enough to get and keep forward movement. Once you begin to sort out what you value and give those activities your attention, you'll feel more in control of your time.

Chapter 4: Taking Action

"The secret of getting ahead is getting started."

Mark Twain

Now that you've identified what really matters to you and you're buzzing with the energy to find balance, it's time to jump right in and take action.

Cyril's Story

Cyril wanted more time with his family. His wife and three boys wanted more time with him. His job as an Information Systems Engineer consumed 50-60 hours of his week, and there was little room for that to change unless he wanted to take a pay cut or lose his seniority, which he didn't.

Cyril followed all the *Balance Your Life* steps. He kept a Feelings Journal; he deepened his self-awareness, took a good long look at what he could let go of and even prioritized his evening and weekend activities, putting family at the top of his list of priorities.

He stopped volunteering to cover for co-workers in the evenings so he could get home and have dinner with his family no less than three nights a week. He realized that was not an area where he was being evaluated for performance, and it wasn't adding to Cyril's sense of well-being. Cyril even limited his Sunday afternoon card games with the guys to two Sundays a month so he could have more family time.

Cyril and his family noticed and loved the difference. He was driving his boys to soccer practice on Saturdays *and* staying to watch and cheer them on. The small repairs around the house he'd been promising were getting done, and he and his wife were bringing in a baby sitter once a week so they could go on a date.

Months later, however, Cyril was back to feeling like his time wasn't his own and the things that mattered weren't getting his attention.

During a coaching session, Cyril revealed that he had made friends with some of the parents at the soccer games. When they found out what he did for a living, several of his new friends were asking for technology help. Cyril, wanting to be a good friend, said yes, and kept saying yes, when approached.

It happened so incrementally that he hadn't noticed his cherished time had been usurped by other activities.

Maintaining Your Balance

As Cyril discovered, doing a friend a one-time favor does not constitute a standing contract that you are their go-to person whenever their computer acts up. It's wonderful when people value your expertise. That doesn't mean you have to give it freely, at someone else's convenience or when it wrecks havoc with your own schedule.

As you continue on this journey to find and maintain balance, I suggest the following essential beliefs. You can tape these where you can see them, or read them often as a gentle reminder that you have taken control of your time and are acting in your best interest.

#1: Your time is valuable

Every day you make an effort to meet deadlines at work, get to appointments on time or pick up your kids from day care before their closing time. In other words, you respect the schedules that other people set. Your time deserves the same respect.

Carve out time that you can contribute to balancing your Self and your relationships. Guard and honor this time and do not let distractions intrude. If some task arises, ask yourself: Why do I need to tend to this new task right now? Does this really matter to me? What will happen if I don't do this right now?

Setting boundaries is essential in protecting what you value. When you value your own time, others learn to value your time as well.

#2: "No" is not a four-letter word

Many of us find it difficult to say no, so we end up taking on tasks that sometimes interfere with more important aspects of our lives, and then feel resentful, guilty, or both. That's not healthy for your holistic Self.

You have control of your time. If you choose to give up your time, then do so freely and without guilt, but figure out what else you're willing to shift or let go so you don't over-schedule yourself.

If you choose not to give up your time, try saying, "I'm sorry. I can't take that on right now and give it the attention and energy it deserves."

People accept an honest response of "no" just as you would accept hearing it to your request. They're probably just trying to get things done too.

If a person escalates a request for your time to a situation rife with confrontation— for example, being annoyingly persistent, arguing your availability, or insisting on a more valid reason for your unavailability— you'll have to be firm. You might explain briefly that your schedule is full, offer an alternative time when you can help him, or, in extreme cases, decide whether or not he is someone you want in your network of support.

#3: Do what you say you'll do

First Century BC, Latin writer Publilius Syrus is noted for saying, "Never promise more than you can perform."

In addition to gaining the reputation of being a person of your word, it's important to your overall well-being that you take control of your time and honor your commitments.

When you commit to accomplishing what you identify as a priority, others will see that you honor your time and begin to honor your time as well. Your actions will show others the person you choose to be and reinforces your sense of Self.

#4: Value your valued relationships

Managing your relationships is not a walk in the park. There are hundreds of thousands of books, blogs, TV programs, and newsletters that cover the subject and offer tips and suggestions for dealing with any given interpersonal situation.

In some situations, if you don't make time for people who are important to you, they may in turn learn to not make time for you.

If a valued person wants your time and you don't have it to give, talk to that individual. Make arrangements to get together and spend quality time in the near future. Good relationships take time and effort, and they're worth it.

#5: Teach people how to treat you

With every interaction, your friends and family learn your likes, dislikes, moods and habits. You learn the same from them. Being consistent is the key to teaching people how to treat you. When you value your time, people learn to value your time.

If you allow someone to consistently usurp your valuable time, you're the one to blame. You've taught that person that you say "yes" whether it's convenient for you or not.

#6: Busy does not mean productive

Busy and productive are not synonyms. When you're busy, you have a full plate of activities. When you're productive you are attending to urgent and/or important tasks and getting them done.

Spend the majority of your personal time engaging in meaningful activities that nourish your life. Ask yourself the following questions, making certain that you answer them honestly.

Will (insert whatever task you are currently facing) add to my well-being? Can it wait until tomorrow or the next day? Can someone else do that while I attend to what matters more?

Taking control of your time means that you are productive throughout your day, not just busy.

#7: Be flexible

New things, situations, or people pop into our lives almost every day. That's a part of life that makes it so challenging, interesting, and exciting.

Don't get frazzled by the unexpected. You are in control of your time. If a new priority emerges, then remember that something on your to-do list loses a little of its priority status. Let that item go or reach for your trusty network list.

Procrastination

"Procrastination is the thief of time."

Edward Young

Many of us are guilty of procrastinating in one form or another. We simply find reasons *not* to do things and that is one of the biggest obstacles to taking control of your time.

People generally procrastinate because a task isn't interesting or it feels impossibly large and impossible to do well in the time you have allotted. If something doesn't pique your interest, consider finding someone else to do it.

If you determine that it is something you must handle yourself, then try making it more interesting. Perhaps you can combine something you enjoy along with the task such as play music you enjoy or get your children involved.

The solution for working past procrastination of a monumental task is to break it down. Start with smaller tasks that you can do in the time you have available.

When you've lived in your home for over a decade, maybe clearing the garage is about as exciting as having a tooth extracted without Novocain. Here's an example of how you can create palatable tasks from that Herculean task.

Task 1: Move all tools in the garage into a storage tub.

Task 2: Taking a tip from the popular show *Clean House*, label the four corners of the garage "keep", "sell", "charity" and "trash."

Task 3: Move what you know you want to keep to the "keep" corner.

Task 4: Move all other items in the garage to their appropriately labeled corner.

Task 4: Get rid of the items marked "trash."

Task 5: If you're anything like the rest of us, you'll want to go through the "keep" pile again. If an item isn't in working order or doesn't have a place in your home or has no real sentimental value to you, consider moving it to a different pile.

Task 6: Call the Salvation Army or your local charity and arrange a pick up of the "charity" pile or load them in the car and drop them off.

Task 7: Plan a garage sale for the "sell" items. Kids love being a part of flea markets. Get them involved.

Maybe some of your neighbors want to do a garage sale as well. You can do it together and have a neighborhood flea market day.

Sharing the to-do's involved in staging a garage sale helps you to build neighborly relationships and provides more people who can take on various tasks.

Task 8: Once your garage is cleared out, you can re-organize it to your liking and needs.

Whenever you feel procrastination zapping your energy and efforts to balance your life, take a deep breath and consider what it might take to motivate you to take action.

Chapter 5: Evaluating Your Progress

"Follow effective action with quiet reflection. From the quiet reflection will come even more effective action."

Peter F. Drucker

When you engage in any sort of behavior change, it's important to take stock of the actions you've elected to use. Evaluating the outcomes of your progress can help to clarify what's important and whether your real needs are being met. It keeps you aware, and that awareness generates more energy.

You may be unaccustomed to self-reflection or internal assessment of new behaviors. You might also be unfamiliar with actively seeking external feedback from others to hear how your actions are being perceived and experienced.

Remember Cyril's story? When he gave away the new found control of his time, his wife and sons did speak up. They noticed the time he'd been spending with them was dwindling again and expressed sadness or disappointment.

Cyril was uncertain what to do about it, so his family's feedback registered as complaints instead of useful information for evaluating his progress. Fortunately, Cyril's conversations with his life coach helped him open up to self-reflection and hearing others' feedback.

Self-reflection and getting feedback takes practice, but here is how you can take stock of the changes you make and maintain balance in your life.

Self-Reflection and Internal Assessment

Self-evaluation helps ensure that you are honoring what matters. Here are some important questions you should ask yourself three or four weeks into making changes to your actions, behavior, or beliefs:

Have I made a difference in my overall well-being? How am I feeling?

Sit quietly and notice what's going on with you physically, emotionally, and mentally. Occasionally, even if there is no sign of anxiety or distress, it's helpful to scan your thoughts, emotions and physical well-being. You'll learn to recognize atypical sensations easier as you practice.

Don't forget to jot your observations in your Feelings Journal. What you can't see today, you might be able to see by revisiting your journal at a later time.

Are the new behaviors getting results?

Do you feel more in control of your time? Are you doing the things you want to do, the things that matter most to you? Are you feeling more balanced?

The outcome you desire is clear—balance in your life. If you aren't feeling more balanced, consider enlisting additional help. Large or complex change takes more thought, planning and preparation than you can manage alone. When it comes to changing a lifetime of habit or self-defeating beliefs, a life coach or other professional support can go a long way toward your ultimate success.

Can I do more? Can what I'm doing now be improved upon?

Perhaps the changes you've made to take control of your time were just the first small step. That's fine. It's wonderful, in fact. You're moving toward a goal of making time for what's most important to you, and every journey starts with a single step.

If what you are doing is working, and you're feeling the results, enjoy and celebrate your success. It's important to celebrate your achievements. It goes a long way toward building confidence, energy, and motivation to keep the new changes on a forward path.

If, after a week or so, you're still feeling out of balance, revisit the *Now vs. Ideal* or the *Juggling Act* sections of this book. Remember, it generally takes 21-60 days for a new behavior to take root in the human consciousness. Give yourself the gift of time to acclimate. Bask in the glow of your current success before reaching for more.

Getting Feedback from Others

Assessing yourself can be difficult for some people. It isn't that you'll deceive yourself on purpose, but often when we want something deeply, we tend to let our enthusiasm color our perceptions of reality. Therefore, it's important to get feedback from the people around you.

It may also be difficult to hear feedback. You might start to feel defensive—especially if the feedback is not as positive as you had hoped. Resist becoming defensive. You should value this information. You *need* it to effectively evaluate your progress.

Following are two examples of methods to get information from others when assessing your progress. You might choose to do one or both depending on what is most comfortable for you.

1. Ask for written, anonymous feedback.

It's important that the people you approach for feedback feel open enough to give their honest input. The people who care most about you, and whom you care about, want to help and support you, not to mislead you, or tell you only what they perceive you want to hear.

Select four to six people in your life and let them know that you are seeking feedback on the changes you've made in your life. Tell them they don't have to write their names on the feedback sheet or identify themselves in any way. Then ask them to respond to the questions you give them. I've included some sample questions in the Appendix that you might want to use, as written, or use as a springboard for your own.

When you get written feedback from others, it's vital that you absorb it as openly and non-defensively as possible.

Schedule time to sit quietly, alone without distraction. Relax, letting go of any thoughts or expectations. This is information that is for your benefit, your well-being, and life balance.

Quietly read through the feedback. Absorb it before you consider your own self-assessment in the mix. You want ultimately to look at the feedback as a whole.

2. Have a dialogue with someone close to you.

This is not intended to be an inquisition or an interview. Dialogue is give and take exchange. You don't want to volley the person with a list of questions like an investigative journalist trying to uncover the truth. That style of interviewing tends to nudge people into a defensive mode.

Instead, share what you've been experiencing. You want to open up dialogue about the changes you've made and get the person's input on their experience of your new behaviors. You can use the written questions mentioned in the first example as a guide for your dialogue.

When the person shares his/her feedback, really listen and take in what he/she is saying. You don't have to *do* anything, just listen and absorb.

Allow yourself to sit in non-judgment and be an observer. If it helps, pretend you're talking about someone else; just make sure you're hearing what the person is saying. It might help to repeat what you heard and get confirmation or clarification.

When the conversation closes, thank the person for speaking and sharing with you. Wait until you are alone to jot down notes, think about the dialogue you had, and plan on how you will best utilize the information you received to your benefit in achieving balance.

Active Listening

Active listening engages every aspect of your being: mind, body, heart, spirit and how you relate to others. It involves hearing what's being said and speaking *solely* to get confirmation or clarity. When you are actively listening, you aren't thinking about a response; you're thinking about the message of the speaker. You control your emotions so that nothing gets in the way of the message being given to you.

It takes some practice, but learning to actively listen is a skill that will serve you well. It has great long-term rewards. You hear the intended message, the speaker feels heard and valued, you create a deeper bond with the speaker, and you get the feedback needed to gauge progress.

When you elect to have a face-to-face dialogue with someone to get feedback, be mindful of your body language. Sit facing the individual without crossing your arms or legs. During interpersonal communication—that is, a dialogue between two people—crossing your appendages puts out the message that you may be closed off or guarded

Conclusion

Sustaining balance in your life is a lifelong journey. New experiences, events, people, situations, and tasks crop up all the time. These new things may prove to be obstacles in maintaining control of your time. Be assured that the solution to keeping control is in knowing what's important to you.

When you elect to change the way you approach personal day-to-day tasks, the steps outlined in this book are ideal for you. Pay attention to the sensations you're feeling. Let them lead you to awareness of what parts of your Self need attention. Deepen your self-awareness and knowledge of what matters most to you. Let go of what doesn't matter, and let the momentum of attending to what's really important carry you forward.

Keep this BALANCE checklist visible and within easy reach to be reminded that YOU are in control of your time and therefore able to maintain the balance you seek.

BALANCE checklist

☐ **B**reathe: Intentional breathing is the fastest way to reconnect the parts of your being: mind, body, heart, spirit and bonds (relationships).

☐ **A**sk: There's a lot you may not know. Be proactive and inquire about the things that interest you. Ask others what they care about; it helps you to appreciate what matters to you.

☐ **L**earn: Whether it's fixing a bike or car, learning a musical instrument, astrophysics or how to cook, the challenge and satisfaction of learning can be fun, build confidence, and feed your mind.

☐ **A**ct: Work past procrastination. To the degree that you are able, maintain mobility and fitness.

☐ **N**urture: Helping others links your happiness to a wider community and is deeply rewarding and spiritual.

☐ **C**onnect: Developing healthy relationships with family, friends, colleagues and neighbors will enrich your life and provide a network of support.

☐ **E**mote: Express your unique self with confidence. Don't be afraid to find your inner voice and use it.

Appendix

The following resources can be used at your leisure. For the two exercises listed, give yourself time to reflect and think about your responses, then record them in the appropriate spaces.

For more information about balance, well-being and other helpful resources, please visit my website:
<u>www.2YourWell-Being.com</u>.

Now vs. Ideal

This exercise helps give a visual of what you are doing now versus what you would like to be doing. When you establish control of your time, you will be able to shift toward doing things in the "Ideal" category by letting go of ineffective or unsupportive activities in the "Now" category.

In the first column, list two to three repetitive activities in each area of your life. In the second column, list two to three activities you would love to do.

	NOW	IDEAL
Career/Work		
Education		
Entertainment		
Environment		
Family/Friends		
Finances		
Health		
Recreation		
Significant Other		
Spirituality		
Other		

Juggling Act

Label each ball you currently juggle as well as each ball that you have dropped or may be waiting to be picked up and added to your juggling act. Include people, situations, problems, changes, or pressures you are juggling, need to juggle, or have dropped. Be as specific as you can when you label.

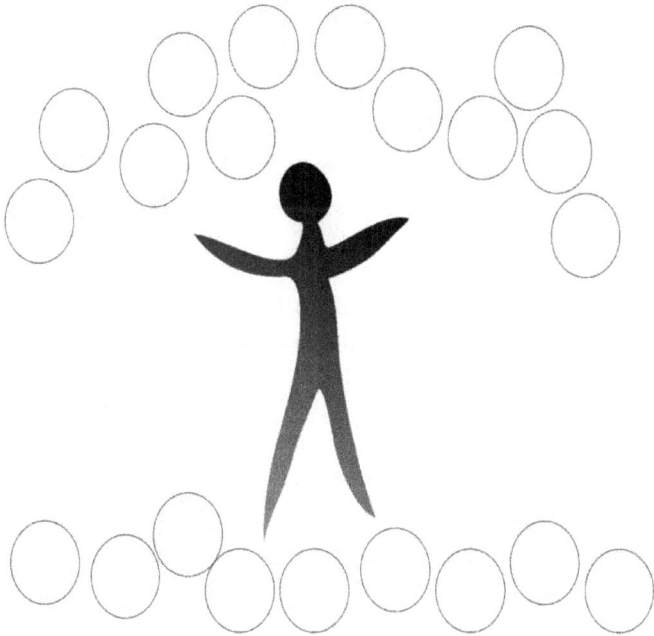

Once you've completed your Juggling Act chart, answer the following questions honestly.

- How do you feel about the total number of balls you're juggling?

- How do you feel about the balls you've dropped?

- Did you drop them out of necessity or without much thought?

- Look at each ball individually. How do you feel about it?

- Is it something you want to continue juggling or leave on the ground?

- Is it something you can control?

- What benefit do you get from keeping this one in the air or out of the air?

- What if any distress does it cause you?

Once you've responded to these questions, make a decision about the number of balls you'll juggle today and which items those are. Remember, you are taking control of your time. You want to select the balls/tasks that will give you a sense of well-being and balance in your life. Create a list.

Next, prioritize the list of activities that you want to attend to today.

And finally, take action.

Evaluating Your Progress – Feedback Sheet

Here is a list of questions you might want to ask or give to the people who have agreed to give you feedback.

1. What new or different things have you noticed about my behavior and actions in the past two to three weeks?

2. What new or different things have you noticed about my overall attitude in the past two to three weeks?

3. What impact have these new and different things had on you?

4. What else would you like to share with me?

When you receive their responses, schedule some quiet time to absorb or read your feedback. Don't forget to include your self-assessment in the data.

Sit and reflect on the information. Scan your reactions: mind, body, heart and spirit. Jot notes in your Feelings Journal. Then decide how you will incorporate the feedback going forward.

2 Your Well-Being

There's only one you, and only so many hours outside of work that you can give your time and talents to yourself and others.

When you know what matters most, you can take control of your time and release the stress-causing time-wasters to make more room for the things that add to your well-being.

Sometimes, you need the support only a life coach can provide.

↳ Be your best so you can you give others your best!

↳ Focus your personal time on what matters most!

↳ Get affordable coaching to balance your life!

2YourWell-Being is a coaching practice that will help you regain control of your time. I can help you focus and work through the life changes you need to make to find more balance and establish a sense of well-being.

Visit my website, www.2YourWell-Being.com, for more information and for free activities that can help you identify what's most important to you so you can take control of your time.

www.ingramcontent.com/pod-product-compliance
Lightning Source LLC
Chambersburg PA
CBHW071421040426
42445CB00012BA/1250